POPE  S

A Little Golden Book® Biography

By Suzanne Slade

Illustrated by Sue Cornelison

A GOLDEN BOOK • NEW YORK

Text copyright © 2024 by Suzanne Slade
Cover art and interior illustrations copyright © 2024 by Sue Cornelison
All rights reserved. Published in the United States by Golden Books, an imprint of
Random House Children's Books, a division of Penguin Random House LLC, 1745 Broadway,
New York, NY 10019. Golden Books, A Golden Book, A Little Golden Book, the G colophon,
and the distinctive gold spine are registered trademarks of Penguin Random House LLC.
rhcbooks.com
Educators and librarians, for a variety of teaching tools, visit us at RHTeachersLibrarians.com
Library of Congress Control Number: 2023951461
ISBN 978-0-593-70832-3 (trade) — ISBN 978-0-593-70833-0 (ebook)
Printed in the United States of America
10 9 8 7 6 5 4 3 2 1

Pope Francis is the head of the Roman Catholic Church and the spiritual leader of more than a billion people around the world.

Like many popes before him, Pope Francis lives in Vatican City, a small country in the middle of Rome, Italy. But he was born in Buenos Aires, Argentina, on December 17, 1936. Named Jorge Mario Bergoglio by his Italian immigrant parents, he was the oldest of five children.

Jorge's family lived in a large Italian community in Buenos Aires. Though Spanish is the official language in Argentina, they spoke Italian with their neighbors and friends. His grandparents, aunts, uncles, and cousins also lived nearby. On Sundays, Jorge and his family attended their local Catholic church. Afterward, they enjoyed a big meal with lots of pasta for everyone.

Jorge was very close to his grandma Rosa. She had great faith in God and shared her faith with Jorge by telling him about the saints and teaching him how to pray. She read Jorge stories, which led to his love of books. And she encouraged him to help those in need.

Jorge was a good student. His favorite subject was science. He liked to dance—especially the tango. After school, Jorge played soccer with his friends at a nearby park.

   As a teenager, Jorge attended school to learn about food and nutrition. In the morning, he worked in a laboratory and performed tests on food. In the afternoon, he took classes in chemistry and other subjects.

One spring day, when Jorge was seventeen years old, he went to his neighborhood church and was surprised to see a priest he hadn't met before.

As they talked, Jorge had a feeling that he should commit his life to God. The feeling was so strong, he decided that, one day, he would become a priest.

Two years later, Jorge entered seminary, a school that teaches people to be priests. He studied and learned more about God, his faith, and religion.

When Jorge was twenty-one, he became sick with pneumonia. The illness damaged his lungs. To save Jorge's life, a doctor removed part of one of his lungs. He had a long and painful recovery. But that difficult experience strengthened his faith in God.

Jorge wanted to be a special kind of priest called a Jesuit. Jesuit priests believe education and learning are important. They choose to live simple lives, spending little money on themselves and giving to people in need. That lifestyle felt right to Jorge.

To become a Jesuit, Jorge had to study for a long time. He attended schools in Chile and Argentina for several years. He also taught at religious schools. The students liked his sense of humor.

In 1969, Jorge became a priest, and people began calling him Father Bergoglio. As a priest, he preached at Mass on Sundays. He spent much of his time helping the poor, sick, and elderly. His kindness and prayers eased their suffering.

Father Bergoglio became a bishop in 1992. His assignment was to help priests in Buenos Aires. He also visited families living in low-income areas of the city. He listened to their problems, blessed their homes, and gave them hope.

Six years later, Bergoglio was named archbishop of Buenos Aires. As archbishop, he had more responsibilities, but his kind heart didn't let him forget about people in need.

Bergoglio was named a cardinal in 2001. He continued to live in Buenos Aires, but now his job included assisting the pope, the leader of the entire Catholic Church. In 2013, Pope Benedict XVI announced he was too old to serve as pope. Bergoglio and other cardinals gathered at the Sistine Chapel in Vatican City to discuss who should be the next pope. Then they voted.

After the votes were counted, white smoke rose from the Sistine Chapel's chimney—that meant a new pope had been elected. It was Bergoglio! The crowd cheered!

Every newly elected pope chooses a new name for himself. Bergoglio chose Francis, after Saint Francis of Assisi, who devoted his life to helping those in need and caring for animals.

Pope Francis was the first pope to pick the name Francis. But those weren't his only "firsts." He was the first pope from South America. And he was the first Jesuit pope.

Though Pope Francis is the most powerful person in the Catholic Church, he continues to live as he always has—simply. Instead of moving into the Vatican's palace, where popes usually stay, he chose to live in a two-room apartment.

Pope Francis has a very busy schedule. On most days, he gets up early to pray for two hours. He then performs morning Mass at the Santa Marta Chapel in the Vatican. After breakfast, he starts his daily work. He may discuss projects to improve local communities or meet with world leaders.

Pope Francis is known as the People's Pope because he loves and cares for all people. He offers advice to presidents, and he blesses prisoners. He is the first pope to invite women to share their votes and opinions at important church meetings.

In Vatican City, he often goes to St. Peter's Square to greet the large crowds who gather to see him. Sometimes he waves to them from his Popemobile, a special vehicle made just for the pope.

Pope Francis provides hope, peace, and inspiration to people around the world.